Mukhtasar al-Akhdari

Mukhtasar al-Akhdari

Summary on 'Ibadat
according to
The School of Imam Malik

by
Sayyidi 'Abd ar-Rahman al-Akhdari
(920/1514 – 953/1546)

Translated by
Aisha Bewley

Classical and Contemporary Books on Islam and Sufism

Copyright © Diwan Press Ltd., 2019 CE/1440 AH

Mukhtasar al-Akhdari

Published by:	Diwan Press Ltd.
	311 Allerton Road
	Bradford
	BD15 7HA
	UK
Website:	www.diwanpress.com
E-mail:	info@diwanpress.com

All rights reserved. No part of this publication may be reproduced, stored in any retrieval system or transmitted in any form or by any means, electronic, mechanical, photocopying, recording or otherwise without the prior permission of the publishers.

Author:	'Abd ar-Rahman al-Akhdari
Translation:	Aisha Bewley
Edited by:	Abdalhaqq Bewley

A catalogue record of this book is available from the British Library.

ISBN-13:	978-1-908892-78-2 (paperback)

Contents

I. The Primary Obligations of a Muslim   2
  Preconditions for Repentance   2
  Unlawful Matters   6

II. Purification   10
  1. Removing Impurity   10
  2. *Wudu'* (Minor Ablution)   12
    The Seven Obligatory Elements of *Wudu'*   12
    Sunnas of *Wudu'*   14
    Meritorious Elements of *Wudu'*   16
  3. Things that Break *Wudu'*   18
    Things that Ritually Break *Wudu'*   18
    Actual Causes   20
  4. Things forbidden when not in *Wudu'*   22
  5. *Ghusl* (Major Ablution)   22
    Obligatory Elements of *Ghusl*   24
    Sunnas of *Ghusl*   24
    Meritorious Elements of *Ghusl*   26
    What is Forbidden in the state of *Janaba*   28
  6. *Tayammum*   28

Obligatory Elements of *Tayammum*	30
Sunnas of *Tayammum*	32
Meritorious Elements of *Tayammum*	32
What Invalidates *Tayammum*	32
7. Menstruation	34
8. Lochia (Bleeding after Childbirth)	36

III. The Prayer 40
1. Times of Prayer 40
   Times when no *nafila* prayers may be done 42
2. Preconditions of the Prayer 42
3. Obligatory Elements of the Prayer 46
4. Precondition of the Intention 48
5. Sunnas of the Prayer 48
6. Meritorious Elements of the Prayer 52
7. Disliked Things in the Prayer 54
   Section 56
   Section 58
8. Making up Prayers 62
9. On Forgetfulness 64
   Forgetfulness in the *Nafila* 86
   Forgetfulness on the part of the Imam 88

بسم الله الرحمن الرحيم

IN THE NAME OF ALLAH, ALL-MERCIFUL,
MOST MERCIFUL

﴿تِلْكَ حُدُودُ اللَّهِ فَلَا تَعْتَدُوهَا﴾

*These are Allah's limits,
so do not overstep them.*
(Surat al-Baqara 2:229)

Praise belongs to Allah, the Lord of all the Worlds, and blessings and peace be upon our master Muhammad, the Seal of the Prophets and the Imam of the Messengers

I. THE PRIMARY OBLIGATIONS OF A MUSLIM

1. To have sound faith

2. To know how to properly carry out individual obligations, such as the judgments regarding the prayer, purification and fasting

3. To observe the limits (*hudud*) imposed by Allah, and hold to His commands and prohibitions and turn in repentance to Allah All-Glorious before He becomes angry.

PRECONDITIONS FOR REPENTANCE

1. Regret for what you did

الْحَمْدُ لِلَّهِ رَبِّ الْعَالَمِينَ وَالصَّلَاةُ وَالسَّلَامُ عَلَى سَيِّدِنَا مُحَمَّدٍ خَاتِمِ النَّبِيِّينَ وَإِمَامِ الْمُرْسَلِينَ

أَوَّلُ مَا يَجِبُ عَلَى الْمُكَلَّفِ

تَصْحِيحُ إِيمَانِهِ

ثُمَّ مَعْرِفَةُ مَا يُصْلِحُ بِهِ فَرْضَ عَيْنِهِ كَأَحْكَامِ الصَّلَاةِ وَالطَّهَارَةِ وَالصِّيَامِ

وَيَجِبُ عَلَيْهِ أَنْ يُحَافِظَ عَلَى حُدُودِ اللَّهِ وَيَقِفَ عِنْدَ أَمْرِهِ وَنَهْيِهِ وَيَتُوبَ إِلَى اللَّهِ سُبْحَانَهُ قَبْلَ أَنْ يَسْخَطَ عَلَيْهِ.

وَشُرُوطُ التَّوْبَةِ

النَّدَمُ عَلَى مَا فَاتَ

2. The intention not to revert to the wrong action for the rest of your life

3. To stop the act of disobedience immediately if one is actually doing it. It is not lawful to put off repentance or say, "I will repent when Allah guides me." That is a sign of misery, abandonment by Allah and lack of insight.

4. One must guard the tongue against obscene language and ugly words, and swearing by divorce (e.g. "If I do not do a thing, I will divorce my wife").

5. One must avoid putting down another Muslim, treating him with contempt, cursing him, or frightening him without a legitimate reason.

6. One must guard one's eyes against looking at what is unlawful. It is not lawful to look at a Muslim with a glance which hurts him unless he is impious in which case you should shun him.

7. One must preserve all one's limbs, as much as one can, from blameworthy actions.

I. The Primary Obligations of a Muslim

وَالنِّيَّةُ أَنْ لَا يَعُودَ إِلَى ذَنْبٍ فِيمَا بَقِيَ عَلَيْهِ مِنْ عُمُرِهِ

وَأَنْ يَتْرُكَ الْمَعْصِيَةَ فِي سَاعَتِهَا إِنْ كَانَ مُتَلَبِّسًا بِهَا، وَلَا يَحِلُّ لَهُ أَنْ يُؤَخِّرَ التَّوْبَةَ، وَلَا يَقُولُ: حَتَّى يَهْدِيَنِي اللَّهُ فَإِنَّهُ مِنْ عَلَامَاتِ الشَّقَاءِ وَالْخِذْلَانِ وَطَمْسِ الْبَصِيرَةِ.

وَيَجِبُ عَلَيْهِ حِفْظُ لِسَانِهِ مِنَ الْفَحْشَاءِ وَالْمُنْكَرِ، وَالْكَلَامِ الْقَبِيحِ، وَأَيْمَانِ الطَّلَاقِ.

وَانْتِهَارِ الْمُسْلِمِ وَإِهَانَتِهِ، وَسَبِّهِ وَتَخْوِيفِهِ فِي غَيْرِ حَقٍّ شَرْعِيٍّ.

وَيَجِبُ عَلَيْهِ حِفْظُ بَصَرِهِ عَنِ النَّظَرِ إِلَى الْحَرَامِ، وَلَا يَحِلُّ لَهُ أَنْ يَنْظُرَ إِلَى مُسْلِمٍ بِنَظْرَةٍ تُؤْذِيهِ إِلَّا أَنْ يَكُونَ فَاسِقًا فَيَجِبُ هِجْرَانُهُ.

وَيَجِبُ عَلَيْهِ حِفْظُ جَمِيعِ جَوَارِحِهِ مَا اسْتَطَاعَ.

8. A Muslim must love for Allah and hate for Him, and be pleased for Him and angry for Him, and he must command the right and forbid the wrong.

Unlawful Matters

1. It is unlawful to lie, to slander, carry tales, be arrogant, be proud, show off for the sake of appearance and reputation, to envy, to hate, to see one oneself as better than others, to find fault, to backbite, to mock, or to ridicule.

2. It is unlawful to commit fornication or to look with lust at a woman to whom you are not married or take pleasure in her words; or to consume the property of people without their consent; or to receive money in exchange for intercession or because of a debt; or to delay the prayer until its time has passed.

3. It is unlawful to keep the company of a deviant person (*fasiq*) or to sit with him without necessity.

I. The Primary Obligations of a Muslim

وَأَنْ يُحِبَّ لِلَّهِ وَيُبْغِضَ لَهُ وَيَرْضَى لَهُ وَيَغْضَبَ لَهُ، وَيَأْمُرَ بِالْمَعْرُوفِ وَيَنْهَى عَنِ الْمُنْكَرِ.

وَيَحْرُمُ عَلَيْهِ

الْكَذِبُ وَالْغِيبَةُ وَالنَّمِيمَةُ وَالْكِبْرُ وَالْعُجْبُ وَالرِّيَاءُ وَالسُّمْعَةُ وَالْحَسَدُ وَالْبُغْضُ وَرُؤْيَةُ الْفَضْلِ عَلَى الْغَيْرِ، وَالْهَمْزُ وَاللَّمْزُ وَالْعَبَثُ وَالسُّخْرِيَةُ.

وَالزِّنَا، وَالنَّظَرُ إِلَى الْأَجْنَبِيَّةِ، وَالتَّلَذُّذُ بِكَلَامِهَا، وَأَكْلُ أَمْوَالِ النَّاسِ بِغَيْرِ طِيبِ نَفْسٍ وَالْأَكْلُ بِالشَّفَاعَةِ أَوْ بِالدِّينِ وَتَأْخِيرُ الصَّلَاةِ عَنْ أَوْقَاتِهَا.

وَلَا يَحِلُّ لَهُ صُحْبَةُ فَاسِقٍ، وَلَا مُجَالَسَتُهُ لِغَيْرِ ضَرُورَةٍ.

4. You should not seek to please creatures at the expense of incurring the anger of the Creator. Allah Almighty says: *"It would be more fitting for them to please Allah and His Messenger if they are believers."* (9:62) The Prophet ﷺ said, "There is no obedience owed to a creature when it involves disobedience of the Creator."

5. It is not lawful to do an action until you know what Allah's judgment about it is. You should ask the people of knowledge and imitate those whose who follow the Sunna of Muhammad ﷺ, those who direct people to how to obey Allah and warn people against following Shaytan.

6. A Muslim should not be content to allow himself to do what the spiritually bankrupt are content to do – those who waste their lives obeying other than Allah Almighty. What regret they will suffer! How long they will weep on the Day of Resurrection!

We ask Allah Almighty to give us success in following the Sunna of our Prophet, intercessor and master, Muhammad ﷺ.

I. The Primary Obligations of a Muslim

وَلَا يَطْلُبُ رِضَا الْمَخْلُوقِينَ بِسَخَطِ الْخَالِقِ، قَالَ اللَّهُ سُبْحَانَهُ وَتَعَالَى: ﴿وَاللَّهُ وَرَسُولُهُ أَحَقُّ أَنْ يُرْضُوهُ إِنْ كَانُوا مُؤْمِنِينَ﴾. وَقَالَ عَلَيْهِ الصَّلَاةُ وَالسَّلَامُ: «لَا طَاعَةَ لِمَخْلُوقٍ فِي مَعْصِيَةِ الْخَالِقِ».

وَلَا يَحِلُّ لَهُ أَنْ يَفْعَلَ فِعْلًا حَتَّى يَعْلَمَ حُكْمَ اللَّهِ فِيهِ وَيَسْأَلَ الْعُلَمَاءَ وَيَقْتَدِيَ بِالْمُتَّبِعِينَ لِسُنَّةِ مُحَمَّدٍ صَلَّى اللَّهُ عَلَيْهِ وَسَلَّمَ الَّذِينَ يَدُلُّونَ عَلَى طَاعَةِ اللَّهِ، وَيُحَذِّرُونَ مِنِ اتِّبَاعِ الشَّيْطَانِ.

وَلَا يَرْضَى لِنَفْسِهِ مَا رَضِيَهُ الْمُفْلِسُونَ الَّذِينَ ضَاعَتْ أَعْمَارُهُمْ فِي غَيْرِ طَاعَةِ اللَّهِ تَعَالَى، فَيَا حَسْرَتَهُمْ وَيَا طُولَ بُكَائِهِمْ يَوْمَ الْقِيَامَةِ.

نَسْأَلُ اللَّهَ أَنْ يُوَفِّقَنَا لِاتِّبَاعِ سُنَّةِ نَبِيِّنَا وَشَفِيعِنَا وَسَيِّدِنَا مُحَمَّدٍ صَلَّى اللَّهُ عَلَيْهِ وَسَلَّمَ.

II. Purification

There are two categories of purification:

1. Purification from ritual impurity.

2. Purification from filth.

Both forms of purification are only valid if done with pure and purifying water, that is water whose colour, taste or smell has not been altered by something which is normally separate from it, such as oil, ghee, all grease, dung, soap, filth and other things. There is no harm in earth, mud, salty earth, and other such things.

1. Removing Impurity

When there is known to be an impurity in a specific place, that place must be washed. If it is unclear where the impurity is, then the entire garment should be washed. If someone is unsure

فَصْلٌ فِي الطَّهَارَةِ

اَلطَّهَارَةُ قِسْمَانِ:

طَهَارَةُ حَدَثٍ.

وَطَهَارَةُ خَبَثٍ.

وَلَا يَصِحُّ الْجَمِيعُ إِلَّا بِالْمَاءِ الطَّاهِرِ الْمُطَهِّرِ، وَهُوَ الَّذِي لَمْ يَتَغَيَّرْ لَوْنُهُ أَوْ طَعْمُهُ أَوْ رَائِحَتُهُ بِمَا يُفَارِقُهُ غَالِبًا كَالزَّيْتِ وَالسَّمْنِ وَالدَّسَمِ كُلِّهِ وَالْوَدَجِ وَالصَّابُونِ وَالْوَسَخِ وَنَحْوِهِ، وَلَا بَأْسَ بِالتُّرَابِ وَالْحَمْأَةِ وَالسَّبَخَةِ وَالْآجُرِّ وَنَحْوِهِ.

فَصْلٌ

إِذَا تَعَيَّنَتِ النَّجَاسَةُ غُسِلَ مَحَلُّهَا، فَإِنِ الْتَبَسَتْ غُسِلَ الثَّوْبُ كُلُّهُ. وَمَنْ شَكَّ فِي إِصَابَةِ النَّجَاسَةِ نَضَحَ، وَإِنْ أَصَابَهُ شَيْءٌ شَكَّ فِي نَجَاسَتِهِ فَلَا نَضْحَ عَلَيْهِ، وَمَنْ تَذَكَّرَ النَّجَاسَةَ وَهُوَ فِي

whether impurity has touched a garment or not, he should sprinkle water on it. If something gets on someone and they are not sure whether it is impure or not, they should not sprinkle water on it. If someone remembers having an impurity on themselves while they are praying, they should break off from the prayer, unless they fear that they will miss the time. If someone prays with the impurity out of forgetfulness and then remembers after the *salam*, they should repeat the prayer if it is still within the time.

2. *WUDU'* (MINOR ABLUTION)

The Seven Obligatory Elements of *Wudu'*

1. The intention

2. Washing the face

3. Washing the hands and arms to the elbows

4. Wiping the head

5. Washing the feet to the ankles

II. Purification

الصَّلَاةِ قَطَعَ إِلَّا أَنْ يَخَافَ خُرُوجَ الْوَقْتِ. وَمَنْ صَلَّى بِهَا نَاسِيًا وَتَذَكَّرَ بَعْدَ السَّلَامِ أَعَادَ فِي الْوَقْتِ.

فَصْلٌ

فَرَائِضُ الْوُضُوءِ سَبْعٌ

اَلنِّيَّةُ

وَغَسْلُ الْوَجْهِ

وَغَسْلُ الْيَدَيْنِ إِلَى الْمِرْفَقَيْنِ

وَمَسْحُ الرَّأْسِ

وَغَسْلُ الرِّجْلَيْنِ إِلَى الْكَعْبَيْنِ

6. Rubbing the limbs

7. Continuity

Sunnas of *Wudu'*

1. Washing the hands to the wrists at the beginning of *wudu'*

2. Rinsing the mouth

3. Snuffing water up the nose

4. Blowing it out

5. Returning the hands to the front when wiping the head

6. Wiping the ears

7. Using fresh water for the ears

8. The correct order of the obligatory elements

If someone forgets an obligatory element and remembers it soon afterwards they should do it and then re-do the rest of *wudu'* after it. If a long

II. Purification

وَالدَّلْكُ

وَالْفَوْرُ

وَسُنَنُهُ

غَسْلُ الْيَدَيْنِ إِلَى الْكُوعَيْنِ عِنْدَ الشُّرُوعِ

وَالْمَضْمَضَةُ

وَالِاسْتِنْشَاقُ

وَالِاسْتِنْثَارُ

وَرَدُّ مَسْحِ الرَّأْسِ

وَمَسْحُ الْأُذُنَيْنِ

وَتَجْدِيدُ الْمَاءِ لَهُمَا

وَالتَّرْتِيبُ بَيْنَ الْفَرَائِضِ

وَمَنْ نَسِيَ فَرْضًا مِنْ أَعْضَائِهِ فَإِنْ تَذَكَّرَهُ بِالْقُرْبِ فَعَلَهُ وَمَا بَعْدَهُ، وَإِنْ طَالَ فَعَلَهُ وَحْدَهُ وَأَعَادَ مَا صَلَّى قَبْلَهُ. وَإِنْ تَرَكَ

time has passed, then they do only that element and repeat any prayers they have done since. If they omit a sunna they should do that missing part of *wudu'* but do not have to repeat the prayer.

If someone omits something insignificant, they wash it alone with an intention to do so. If he prayed before that, they must repeat the prayer.

If someone remembers that they forgot to rinse their mouth and snuff water up the nose after they have started to wash their face, they should not go back and do them until they have finished their *wudu'*.

Meritorious Elements of *Wudu'*

1. The *basmala*

2. Using the *siwak* (tooth-stick)

3. Wiping the face and hands more than once

4. Wiping the head beginning with the forehead

5. The correct order of the sunnas

6. Using small quantities of water

II. Purification

سُنَّةٌ فَعَلَها وَلَا يُعِيدُ الصَّلَاةَ.

وَمَنْ نَسِيَ لُمْعَةً غَسَلَها وَحْدَها بِنِيَّةٍ وَإِنْ صَلَّى قَبْلَ ذَلِكَ أَعَادَ.

وَمَنْ تَذَكَّرَ الْمَضْمَضَةَ وَالِاسْتِنْشَاقَ بَعْدَ أَنْ شَرَعَ فِي الْوَجْهِ فَلَا يَرْجِعُ إِلَيْهِمَا حَتَّى يُتِمَّ وُضُوءَهُ.

وَفَضَائِلُهُ

التَّسْمِيَةُ

وَالسِّوَاكُ

وَالزَّائِدُ عَلَى الْغَسْلَةِ الْأُولَى فِي الْوَجْهِ وَالْيَدَيْنِ

وَالْبُدَاءَةُ بِمُقَدَّمِ الرَّأْسِ

وَتَرْتِيبُ السُّنَنِ

وَقِلَّةُ الْمَاءِ عَلَى الْعُضْوِ

7. Starting with the right before the left

Water must go between the fingers and it is recommended for it to go between the toes.

Water must be made to penetrate a thin beard in *wudu'* but it is not necessary in the case of a thick beard. Water must penetrate the beard in *ghusl*, even if it is thick.

3. Things that Break *Wudu'*

Breaking *wudu'* can ensue from ritual impurity or actual causes.

Things that Ritually Break *Wudu'*

1. Urine

2. Defecation

3. Breaking wind

4. Emission of prostatic fluid and genital discharge

II. Purification

وَتَقْدِيمُ الْيُمْنَى عَلَى الْيُسْرَى

وَيَجِبُ تَخْلِيلُ أَصَابِعِ الرِّجْلَيْنِ.

وَيَجِبُ تَخْلِيلُ اللِّحْيَةِ الْخَفِيفَةِ فِي الْوُضُوءِ دُونَ الْكَثِيفَةِ،

وَيَجِبُ تَخْلِيلُهَا فِي الْغُسْلِ وَلَوْ كَانَتْ كَثِيفَةً.

فَصْلٌ

نَوَاقِضُ الْوُضُوءِ أَحْدَاثٌ وَأَسْبَابٌ:

فَالْأَحْدَاثُ

الْبَوْلُ

وَالْغَائِطُ

وَالرِّيحُ

وَالْمَذْيُ وَالْوَدْيُ

Actual Causes

1. Heavy sleep
2. Unconsciousness
3. Intoxication
4. Insanity
5. Kissing
6. Touching a woman if sexual pleasure is either intended or experienced.
7. Touching the penis with the inside of the palm or the inside of the fingers.

If someone is unsure about having broken *wudu'* they must do *wudu'* again, unless it is a matter of whispering originating from Shaytan, in which case they do not have to do anything.

If prostatic fluid emerges, the entire penis must be washed but not the testicles.

Prostatic fluid is a liquid which can be produced by sexual thoughts, looks or other causes.

II. Purification

وَالْأَسْبَابُ

النَّوْمُ الثَّقِيلُ

وَالْإِغْمَاءُ

وَالسُّكْرُ

وَالْجُنُونُ

وَالْقُبْلَةُ

وَلَمْسُ الْمَرْأَةِ إِنْ قَصَدَ اللَّذَّةَ أَوْ وَجَدَهَا

وَمَسُّ الذَّكَرِ بِبَاطِنِ الْكَفِّ أَوْ بِبَاطِنِ الْأَصَابِعِ

وَمَنْ شَكَّ فِي حَدَثٍ وَجَبَ عَلَيْهِ الْوُضُوءُ إِلَّا أَنْ يَكُونَ مُوَسْوَسًا فَلَا شَيْءَ عَلَيْهِ.

وَيَجِبُ عَلَيْهِ غَسْلُ الذَّكَرِ كُلِّهِ مِنَ الْمَذْيِ، وَلَا يَغْسِلُ الْأُنْثَيَيْنِ.

وَالْمَذْيُ هُوَ الْمَاءُ الْخَارِجُ عِنْدَ الشَّهْوَةِ الصُّغْرَى بِتَفَكُّرٍ أَوْ نَظَرٍ أَوْ غَيْرِهِ.

4. Things forbidden when not in *Wudu'*

It is not lawful for someone who is not in *wudu'* to pray, do *tawaf*, touch a copy of the Qur'an or its cover with his hand or a stick or the like, although there is an allowance for someone who is learning it. A Qur'an writing board may not be touched without *wudu'* except in the case of a student or a teacher who needs to correct it. The ruling for a child touching the Qur'an is the same as that for adults. The sin belongs to the one who hands it to the child not in *wudu'*.

Whoever prays deliberately without *wudu'* is an unbeliever – may Allah preserve us!

5. *Ghusl* (Major Ablution)

Ghusl is obliged on account of three things: *janaba*, menstruation and lochia.

There are two causes of *janaba*:

1. One is the emission of sperm with normal pleasure while asleep or awake, by means of sexual intercourse or for any other reason.

II. Purification

فَصْلٌ

لَا يَحِلُّ لِغَيْرِ الْمُتَوَضِّئِ صَلَاةٌ وَلَا طَوَافٌ وَلَا مَسُّ نُسْخَةِ الْقُرْآنِ الْعَظِيمِ وَلَا جِلْدِهَا، لَا بِيَدِهِ وَلَا بِعُودٍ وَنَحْوِهِ إِلَّا الْجُزْءَ مِنْهَا الْمُتَعَلِّمِ فِيهِ، وَلَا مَسُّ لَوْحِ الْقُرْآنِ الْعَظِيمِ عَلَى غَيْرِ الْوُضُوءِ إِلَّا لِمُتَعَلِّمٍ فِيهِ أَوْ مُعَلِّمٍ يُصَحِّحُهُ وَالصَّبِيُّ فِي مَسِّ الْقُرْآنِ كَالْكَبِيرِ، وَالْإِثْمُ عَلَى مُنَاوِلِهِ لَهُ.

وَمَنْ صَلَّى بِغَيْرِ وُضُوءٍ عَامِدًا فَهُوَ كَافِرٌ وَالْعِيَاذُ بِاللَّهِ.

فَصْلٌ

يَجِبُ الْغُسْلُ مِنْ ثَلَاثَةِ أَشْيَاءَ: الْجَنَابَةِ وَالْحَيْضِ وَالنِّفَاسِ.

فَالْجَنَابَةُ قِسْمَانِ:
أَحَدُهُمَا خُرُوجُ الْمَنِيِّ بِلَذَّةٍ مُعْتَادَةٍ فِي نَوْمٍ أَوْ يَقَظَةٍ بِجِمَاعٍ أَوْ غَيْرِهِ.

2. The other is the disappearance of the glans of the penis into the vagina.

Anyone who dreams that he is having sex but no sperm issues from him owes nothing. Anyone who finds dry sperm on his clothes but does not know how it got there, should have a *ghusl* and repeat any prayers he has done since the last time he slept.

Obligatory Elements of *Ghusl*

1. The intention at the beginning
2. Continuity
3. Rubbing
4. Washing the entire body

Sunnas of *Ghusl*

1. Washing the hands to the wrists as in *wudu'*
2. Rinsing the mouth
3. Snuffing water up and blowing it out,

II. Purification

وَالثَّانِي: مَغِيبُ الْحَشَفَةِ فِي الْفَرْجِ.

وَمَنْ رَأَى فِي مَنَامِهِ كَأَنَّهُ يُجَامِعُ وَلَمْ يَخْرُجْ مِنْهُ مَنِيٌّ فَلَا شَيْءَ عَلَيْهِ، وَمَنْ وَجَدَ فِي ثَوْبِهِ مَنِيًّا يَابِسًا لَا يَدْرِي مَتَى أَصَابَهُ اغْتَسَلَ وَأَعَادَ مَا صَلَّى مِنْ آخِرِ نَوْمَةٍ نَامَهَا فِيهِ.

فصلٌ: فَرَائِضُ الْغُسْلِ

النِّيَّةُ عِنْدَ الشُّرُوعِ

وَالْفَوْرُ

وَالدَّلْكُ

وَالْعُمُومُ

وَسُنَنُهُ

غَسْلُ الْيَدَيْنِ إِلَى الْكُوعَيْنِ كَالْوُضُوءِ

وَالْمَضْمَضَةُ

وَالِاسْتِنْشَاقُ وَالِاسْتِنْثَارُ

4. Washing the inner parts of the ears. As for the lower lobes of the ears, it is obligatory to wash the front and back of them.

Meritorious Elements of *Ghusl*

1. Beginning by washing away the impurity and then the penis and making the intention at that time.

2. Then washing the limbs as for *wudu'*, one by one, and then the upper part of the body.

3. Washing the head three times

4. Doing the right side first

5. Using a minimum quantity of water.

Anyone who forgets to wash a small area or a limb in their *ghusl*, should wash it when they remember, even after a month has passed, and repeat what they have prayed since. If someone delays doing that after they have remembered, their whole *ghusl* is invalid. If it is a limb that is washed in *wudu'* and it happens to be washed in *wudu'* that is enough.

II. Purification

وَغَسْلُ صِمَاخِ الْأُذُنِ وَهِيَ الثُّقْبَةُ الدَّاخِلَةُ فِي الرَّأْسِ. وَأَمَّا صَحْفَةُ الْأُذُنِ فَيَجِبُ غَسْلُ ظَاهِرِهَا وَبَاطِنِهَا.

وَفَضَائِلُهُ

الْبِدَايَةُ بِغَسْلِ النَّجَاسَةِ ثُمَّ الذَّكَرِ فَيَنْوِي عِنْدَهُ.

ثُمَّ أَعْضَاءِ الْوُضُوءِ مَرَّةً مَرَّةً، ثُمَّ أَعْلَى جَسَدِهِ

وَتَثْلِيثُ غَسْلِ الرَّأْسِ
وَتَقْدِيمُ شِقِّ جَسَدِهِ الْأَيْمَنِ
وَتَقْلِيلُ الْمَاءِ عَلَى الْأَعْضَاءِ.

وَمَنْ نَسِيَ لُمْعَةً أَوْ عُضْوًا مِنْ غُسْلِهِ بَادَرَ إِلَى غَسْلِهِ حِينَ تَذَكُّرِهِ، وَلَوْ بَعْدَ شَهْرٍ، وَأَعَادَ مَا صَلَّى قَبْلَهُ. وَإِنْ أَخَّرَهُ بَعْدَ ذِكْرِهِ بَطَلَ غَسْلُهُ. فَإِنْ كَانَ فِي أَعْضَاءِ الْوُضُوءِ وَصَادَفَهُ غَسْلُ الْوُضُوءِ أَجْزَأَهُ.

What is Forbidden in the state of *Janaba*

It is forbidden for anyone in *janaba* to enter the mosque or recite the Qur'an, except for an *ayat* or so for seeking protection, supplication or the like.

It is forbidden for someone who cannot use cold water to have sex with his wife until he has prepared a vessel with warm water in it. If he has a wet dream, that is not held against him.

6. *Tayammum*

Travellers can do *tayammum* provided the journey they are on is not for the sake of doing something which entails disobedience to Allah and sick people can do it for both *fard* (obligatory) and *nafila* (voluntary) prayers. A healthy person can do *tayammum* for the *fard* prayer if he fears missing the time. A healthy person who is not travelling cannot do *tayammum* for a *nafila* prayer, Jumu'a, or a funeral prayer unless the funeral prayer is a bounden duty on him.

فَصْلٌ

لَا يَحِلُّ لِلْجُنُبِ دُخُولُ الْمَسْجِدِ، وَلَا قِرَاءَةُ الْقُرْآنِ إِلَّا الْآيَةَ وَنَحْوَهَا لِلتَّعَوُّذِ وَنَحْوِهِ.

وَلَا يَجُوزُ لِمَنْ لَا يَقْدِرُ عَلَى الْمَاءِ الْبَارِدِ أَنْ يَأْتِيَ زَوْجَتَهُ حَتَّى يُعِدَّ الْآلَةَ إِلَّا أَنْ يَحْتَلِمَ، فَلَا شَيْءَ عَلَيْهِ.

فَصْلٌ فِي التَّيَمُّمِ

وَيَتَيَمَّمُ الْمُسَافِرُ فِي غَيْرِ مَعْصِيَةٍ، وَالْمَرِيضُ لِفَرِيضَةٍ أَوْ نَافِلَةٍ. وَيَتَيَمَّمُ الْحَاضِرُ الصَّحِيحُ لِلْفَرَائِضِ إِذَا خَافَ خُرُوجَ وَقْتِهَا. وَلَا يَتَيَمَّمُ الْحَاضِرُ الصَّحِيحُ لِنَافِلَةٍ وَلَا جُمُعَةٍ وَلَا جِنَازَةٍ إِلَّا إِذَا تَعَيَّنَتْ عَلَيْهِ الْجِنَازَةُ.

Obligatory Elements of *Tayammum*

1. Intention

2. Pure earth

3. Wiping the face

4. Wiping the hands to the wrists

5. The first strike on the earth

6. Continuity

7. The arrival of the time of the prayer

8. Doing it directly before the prayer.

Earth (*saʿīd*) means actual soil and sand, as well as sun-dried bricks, stones, snow, dirt which has been moved from its original place and other such things.

It is not permitted to perform *tayammum* using whitewashed (or painted) walls, mats, wood, grass or the like. There is an allowance for sick people to use a stone or sun-dried brick wall if they cannot use anything else.

II. Purification

وَفَرَائِضُ التَّيَمُّمِ

النِّيَّةُ

وَالصَّعِيدُ الطَّاهِرُ

وَمَسْحُ الْوَجْهِ

وَمَسْحُ الْيَدَيْنِ إِلَى الْكُوعَيْنِ

وَضَرْبَةُ الْأَرْضِ الْأُولَى

وَالْفَوْرُ

وَدُخُولُ الْوَقْتِ

وَاتِّصَالُهُ بِالصَّلَاةِ.

وَالصَّعِيدُ هُوَ التُّرَابُ وَالطُّوبُ، وَالْحَجَرُ، وَالثَّلْجُ وَالْحَضْحَاضُ وَنَحْوُ ذَلِكَ.

وَلَا يَجُوزُ بِالْجِصِّ الْمَطْبُوخِ وَالْحَصِيرِ وَالْخَشَبِ وَالْحَشِيشِ وَنَحْوِهِ، وَرُخِّصَ لِلْمَرِيضِ فِي حَائِطِ الْحَجَرِ وَالطُّوبِ إِنْ لَمْ يَجِدْ مُنَاوِلًا غَيْرَهُ.

Sunnas of *Tayammum*

1. Striking the earth again for the hands

2. Wiping between the wrists and elbows

3. The correct order.

Meritorious Elements of *Tayammum*

1. The *basmala*

2. Doing the right before the left

3. Doing the outside of the arm before the inside

4. Doing the front before the back.

What Invalidates *Tayammum*

The same things that break *wudu'* break *tayammum*.

You cannot pray two *fard* prayers with the same *tayammum*. If you do *tayammum* for a *fard* prayer, you are permitted to do the nafilas after it as well, touch the copy of the Qur'an, perform *tawaf*, or recite, provided you intended that and

II. Purification

وَسُنَنُهُ

تَجْدِيدُ الصَّعِيدِ لِيَدَيْهِ

وَمَسْحُ مَا بَيْنَ الْكُوعَيْنِ وَالْمِرْفَقَيْنِ

وَالتَّرْتِيبُ.

وَفَضَائِلُهُ

التَّسْمِيَةُ

وَتَقْدِيمُ الْيُمْنَى عَلَى الْيُسْرَى

وَتَقْدِيمُ ظَاهِرِ الذِّرَاعِ عَلَى بَاطِنِهِ

وَمُقَدَّمِهِ عَلَى مُؤَخَّرِهِ.

وَنَوَاقِضُهُ

كَالْوُضُوءِ

وَلَا تُصَلَّى فَرِيضَتَانِ بِتَيَمُّمٍ وَاحِدٍ وَمَنْ تَيَمَّمَ لِفَرِيضَةٍ جَازَ لَهُ النَّوَافِلُ بَعْدَهَا وَمَسُّ الْمُصْحَفِ، وَالطَّوَافُ وَالتِّلَاوَةُ إِنْ نَوَى ذَلِكَ وَاتَّصَلَتْ بِالصَّلَاةِ وَلَمْ يَخْرُجِ الْوَقْتُ.

it is directly connected to the prayer and the time of that prayer has not elapsed.

Tayammum for *nafila* permits all the things mentioned above except the *fard* prayer.

If someone prays the 'Isha' prayer with *tayammum*, they should get up to pray the *shafʿ* and *witr* without delay.

If someone does *tayammum* when in *janaba*, they must make a specific intention for doing that.

7. Menstruation

Women are either:

1. Beginning menstruation

2. Having regular periods

3. Pregnant.

The maximum of length of the period of a woman beginning menstruation is 15 days.

For a woman with a regular period, the

وَجَازَ بِتَيَمُّمِ النَّافِلَةِ كُلُّ مَا ذُكِرَ إِلَّا الْفَرِيضَةَ.

وَمَنْ صَلَّى الْعِشَاءَ بِتَيَمُّمٍ قَامَ لِلشَّفْعِ وَالْوَتْرِ بَعْدَهَا مِنْ غَيْرِ تَأْخِيرٍ.

وَمَنْ تَيَمَّمَ مِنْ جَنَابَةٍ فَلَا بُدَّ مِنْ نِيَّتِهَا.

فَصْلٌ فِي الْحَيْضِ

وَالنِّسَاءُ

مُبْتَدَأَةٌ

وَمُعْتَادَةٌ

وَحَامِلٌ

وَأَكْثَرُ الْحَيْضِ لِلْمُبْتَدَأَةِ خَمْسَةَ عَشَرَ يَوْمًا.

وَلِلْمُعْتَادَةِ عَادَتُهَا. فَإِنْ تَمَادَى بِهَا الدَّمُ زَادَتْ ثَلَاثَةَ أَيَّامٍ مَا

maximum is the length of her normal period plus three days more, as long as that does not exceed 15 days.

For a pregnant woman, the maximum is 15 days when she is more than three months and less than six months pregnant. After six months, it is twenty days. If the bleeding stops, she puts her days together until she completes the time of her normal period.[1]

It is not lawful for a menstruating woman to pray, fast, do *tawaf*, touch the Qur'an or enter a mosque. She must make up the fast but not the prayers. It is permitted for her to recite. Her vagina is not permitted for her husband, nor what is between her waist and knees, until she has had a *ghusl*.

8. Lochia (Bleeding after Childbirth)

Lochia is like menstruation regarding what it prohibits. Its maximum length is 60 days. If the

---

[1] The rules regarding irregular periods vary greatly from one jurist to another. The minimum period of purity between periods is fifteen days.

II. Purification

لَمْ تُجَاوِزْ خَمْسَةَ عَشَرَ يَوْمًا.

وَلِلْحَامِلِ بَعْدَ ثَلَاثَةِ أَشْهُرٍ خَمْسَةَ عَشَرَ يَوْمًا وَنَحْوُهَا، وَبَعْدَ سِتَّةِ أَشْهُرٍ عِشْرُونَ وَنَحْوُهَا، فَإِنْ تَقَطَّعَ الدَّمُ لَفَّقَتْ أَيَّامَهُ حَتَّى تُكَمِّلَ عَادَتَهَا.

وَلَا يَحِلُّ لِلْحَائِضِ صَلَاةٌ وَلَا صَوْمٌ وَلَا طَوَافٌ وَلَا مَسُّ مُصْحَفٍ وَلَا دُخُولُ مَسْجِدٍ. وَعَلَيْهَا قَضَاءُ الصَّوْمِ دُونَ الصَّلَاةِ، وَقِرَاءَتُهَا جَائِزَةٌ، وَلَا يَحِلُّ لِزَوْجِهَا فَرْجُهَا وَلَا مَا بَيْنَ سُرَّتِهَا وَرُكْبَتِيهَا حَتَّى تَغْتَسِلَ.

فَصْلٌ فِي النِّفَاسِ

وَالنِّفَاسُ كَالْحَيْضِ فِي مَنْعِهِ، وَأَكْثَرُهُ سِتُّونَ يَوْمًا، فَإِذَا انْقَطَعَ الدَّمُ قَبْلَهَا وَلَوْ فِي يَوْمِ الْوِلَادَةِ، اغْتَسَلَتْ وَصَلَّتْ فَإِذَا عَاوَدَهَا الدَّمُ فَإِنْ كَانَ بَيْنَهُمَا خَمْسَةَ عَشَرَ يَوْمًا فَأَكْثَرُ كَانَ الثَّانِي حَيْضًا، وَإِلَّا ضُمَّ إِلَى الْأَوَّلِ وَكَانَ مِنْ تَمَامِ النِّفَاسِ.

bleeding ends before that, even if that is only a day after childbirth, then a woman has a *ghusl* and prays. If the bleeding resumes, and there is 15 days or more between them, then the second is considered to be menstruation. Otherwise, it is added to the first, and is considered as part of lochia.

II. Purification

III. The Prayer

1. Times of Prayer

The preferred (*ikhtiyari*) time of Dhuhr is from the time the sun begins to decline until the shadow of an object is equal to its length.

The preferred time of 'Asr is from the end of the time of Dhuhr to the yellowing of the sun. The *daruri* time – the time in which they must be done – of Dhuhr and 'Asr extends until sunset.

The preferred time of Maghrib is the length of time it takes to pray it after its preconditions have been met.

The preferred time of 'Isha' is from the disappearance of red in the sky up until the end of the first third of the night. The *daruri* time of these two prayers extends until dawn.

The preferred time of Subh is from first light until the brightening of the sky, and its *daruri* time extends until sunrise.

فَصْلُ في الأَوْقَاتِ

اَلْوَقْتُ الْمُخْتَارُ لِلظُّهْرِ مِنْ زَوَالِ الشَّمْسِ إِلَى آخَرِ الْقَامَةِ.

وَالْمُخْتَارُ لِلْعَصْرِ مِنْ الْقَامَةِ إِلَى الاصْفِرَارِ وَضَرُورِيُّهُمَا إِلَى الْغُرُوبِ.

وَالْمُخْتَارُ لِلْمَغْرِبِ قَدْرُ مَا تُصَلَّى فِيهِ بَعْدَ شُرُوطِهَا.

وَالْمُخْتَارُ لِلْعَشَاءِ مِنْ مَغِيبِ الشَّفَقِ إِلَى ثُلُثِ اللَّيْلِ الْأَوَّلِ. وَضَرُورِيُّهُمَا إِلَى طُلُوعِ الْفَجْرِ.

وَالْمُخْتَارُ لِلصُّبْحِ مِنَ الْفَجْرِ إِلَى الْإِسْفَارِ الْأَعْلَى وَضَرُورِيُّهُ إِلَى طُلُوعِ الشَّمْسِ.

Performing a prayer outside these times is considered to be making it up.

Anyone who delays the prayer until its time has gone has committed a serious wrong action unless it was due to forgetfulness or because he was asleep.

Times when no *nafila* prayers may be done

1. After the Subh prayer until the sun is high

2. After the 'Asr prayer until the Maghrib prayer

3. After the rising of dawn except for usually performed optional *rak'ahs* (*wird*) if someone has slept without praying them

4. After the Imam of the Jumu'a sits on the minbar

5. After Jumu'a until you have left the mosque.

2. Preconditions of the Prayer

1. Purity from ritual impurity

وَالْقَضَاءُ فِي الْجَمِيعِ مَا وَرَاءَ ذَلِكَ.

وَمَنْ أَخَّرَ الصَّلَاةَ حَتَّى خَرَجَ وَقْتُهَا فَعَلَيْهِ ذَنْبٌ عَظِيمٌ إِلَّا أَنْ يَكُونَ نَاسِيًا أَوْ نَائِمًا.

وَلَا تُصَلَّى نَافِلَةٌ:

بَعْدَ صَلَاةِ الصُّبْحِ إِلَى ارْتِفَاعِ الشَّمْسِ

وَبَعْدَ صَلَاةِ الْعَصْرِ إِلَى صَلَاةِ الْمَغْرِبِ

وَبَعْدَ طُلُوعِ الْفَجْرِ إِلَّا الْوِرْدَ لِنَائِمٍ عَنْهُ

وَعِنْدَ جُلُوسِ إِمَامِ الْجُمْعَةِ عَلَى الْمِنْبَرِ

وَبَعْدَ الْجُمْعَةِ حَتَّى يَخْرُجَ مِنَ الْمَسْجِدِ.

فَصْلٌ فِي شُرُوطِ الصَّلَاةِ

وَشُرُوطُ الصَّلَاةِ طَهَارَةُ الْحَدَثِ

2. Purity from impurities on the body, clothes and place

3. Covering the private parts

4. Facing the *qibla*

5. Not talking

6. Avoidance of multiple extra movements

The private parts of a man are considered to be what is between his navel and his knees. All of a woman is considered to be a private part except her face and palms.

It is disliked for someone to pray in trousers unless there is something over them.

If someone has an impure garment and cannot find another and cannot find water to wash it with, or does not have anything else to wear when they wash it, and they fear missing the time, they should pray in it despite the impurity.

It is not permitted to delay the prayer for want of purity. Whoever does that disobeys his Lord. If someone cannot find anything to cover their private parts, they should pray naked.

III. The Prayer

وَطَهَارَةُ الْخَبَثِ مِنَ الْبَدَنِ وَالثَّوْبِ وَالْمَكَانِ

وَسَتْرُ الْعَوْرَةِ

وَاسْتِقْبَالُ الْقِبْلَةِ

وَتَرْكُ الْكَلَامِ

وَتَرْكُ الْأَفْعَالِ الْكَثِيرَةِ.

وَعَوْرَةُ الرَّجُلِ مَا بَيْنَ السُّرَّةِ وَالرُّكْبَةِ، وَالْمَرْأَةُ كُلُّهَا عَوْرَةٌ مَا عَدَا الْوَجْهَ وَالْكَفَّيْنِ.

وَتُكْرَهُ الصَّلَاةُ فِي السَّرَاوِيلِ، إِلَّا إِذَا كَانَ فَوْقَهَا شَيْءٌ.

وَمَنْ تَنَجَّسَ ثَوْبُهُ وَلَمْ يَجِدْ ثَوْبًا غَيْرَهُ وَلَمْ يَجِدْ مَاءً يَغْسِلُهُ بِهِ أَوْ لَمْ يَكُنْ عِنْدَهُ مَا يَلْبَسُ حَتَّى يَغْسِلَهُ وَخَافَ خُرُوجَ الْوَقْتِ صَلَّى بِنَجَاسَتِهِ.

وَلَا يَحِلُّ تَأْخِيرُ الصَّلَاةِ لِعَدَمِ الطَّهَارَةِ، وَمَنْ فَعَلَ ذَلِكَ فَقَدْ عَصَى رَبَّهُ، وَمَنْ لَمْ يَجِدْ مَا يَسْتُرُ بِهِ عَوْرَتَهُ صَلَّى عُرْيَانًا.

If someone makes a mistake about the direction of the *qibla*, they should repeat the prayer within the time. Every repetition within the time is meritorious. All the prayers can be repeated within the time, but missed prayers and *nafila* prayers should not be repeated.

3. Obligatory Elements of the Prayer

1. The intention for the specific prayer

2. The *takbir al-ihram*

3. Standing for it

4. The Fatiha

5. Standing during it

6. *Ruku'* (bowing)

7. Rising from it

8. Prostration on the forehead

9. Rising from it

وَمَنْ أَخْطَأَ الْقِبْلَةَ أَعَادَ فِي الْوَقْتِ، وَكُلُّ إِعَادَةٍ فِي الْوَقْتِ فَهِيَ فَضِيلَةٌ، وَكُلُّ مَا تُعَادُ مِنْهُ الصَّلَاةُ فِي الْوَقْتِ فَلَا تُعَادُ مِنْهُ الْفَائِتَةُ وَالنَّافِلَةُ.

فَصْلٌ: فَرَائِضُ الصَّلَاةِ

نِيَّةُ الصَّلَاةِ الْمُعَيَّنَةِ

وَتَكْبِيرَةُ الْإِحْرَامِ

وَالْقِيَامُ لَهَا

وَالْفَاتِحَةُ

وَالْقِيَامُ لَهَا

وَالرُّكُوعُ

وَالرَّفْعُ مِنْهُ

وَالسُّجُودُ عَلَى الْجَبْهَةِ

وَالرَّفْعُ مِنْهُ

10. Correctness of the positions

11. Stillness in the positions

12. The correct order of the obligatory elements

13. The *salam*

14. The final sitting which accompanies it.

4. Precondition of the Intention

1. It must accompany the *takbir al-ihram*.

5. Sunnas of the Prayer

1. The *iqama*

2. The *sura* after the Fatiha

3. Standing during it

4. Reciting silently in the silent prayers

5. Reciting aloud in the out-loud prayers

6. Saying "*sami'allahu liman hamidah*"

III. The Prayer

وَالِاعْتِدَالُ

وَالطُّمَانِينَةُ

وَالتَّرْتِيبُ بَيْنَ فَرَائِضِهَا

وَالسَّلَامُ

وَجُلُوسُهُ الَّذِي يُقَارِنُهُ.

وَشَرْطُ النِّيَّةِ

مُقَارَنَتُهَا لِتَكْبِيرَةِ الْإِحْرَامِ.

وَسُنَّتُهَا

الْإِقَامَةُ

وَالسُّورَةُ الَّتِي بَعْدَ الْفَاتِحَةِ

وَالْقِيَامُ لَهَا

وَالسِّرُّ فِيمَا يُسَرُّ فِيهِ

وَالْجَهْرُ فِيمَا يُجْهَرُ فِيهِ

وَسَمِعَ اللهُ لِمَنْ حَمِدَهُ

7. Every *takbir* is sunna except the first one

8-9. The two *tashahhuds* and sitting for them

10. Reciting the Fatiha before the *sura*

11. The second *salam* and a third for the follower

12. Saying the obligatory *taslim* aloud

13. The prayer on the Messenger of Allah ﷺ

14. Prostration on the nose, palms, knees and ends of the toes

15. The *sutra* for anyone other than the one following an imam. Its minimum dimensions are the thickness of a spear and the length of a forearm and it should be something pure, firm and not distracting.[2]

---

2 The *sutra* is something you place in front of you when performing the prayer.

III. The Prayer

وَكُلُّ تَكْبِيرَةٍ سُنَّةٌ إِلَّا الْأُولَى

وَالتَّشَهُّدَانِ وَالْجُلُوسُ لَهُمَا

وَتَقْدِيمُ الْفَاتِحَةِ عَلَى السُّورَةِ

وَالتَّسْلِيمَةُ الثَّانِيَةُ وَالثَّالِثَةُ لِلْمَأْمُومِ

وَالْجَهْرُ بِالتَّسْلِيمَةِ الْوَاجِبَةِ

وَالصَّلَاةُ عَلَى رَسُولِ اللهِ صَلَّى اللهُ عَلَيْهِ وَسَلَّمَ

وَالسُّجُودُ عَلَى الْأَنْفِ وَالْكَفَّيْنِ وَالرُّكْبَتَيْنِ وَأَطْرَافِ الْقَدَمَيْنِ

وَالسُّتْرَةُ لِغَيْرِ الْمَأْمُومِ وَأَقَلُّهَا غِلَظُ رُمْحٍ وَطُولُ ذِرَاعٍ طَاهِرٍ ثَابِتٍ غَيْرِ مُشَوَّشٍ.

6. Meritorious Elements of the Prayer

1. Raising the hands for the *takbir al-ihram* to the level of the ears

2. The words of the follower and the one praying alone: *"rabbana wa laka-l-hamd"*

3. The amen after the Fatiha for the one praying alone and the follower, but the imam only says it in the silent recitation

4. Saying *"subhan'allah"* in *ruku'*

5. Supplication in the prostration

6. Long recitation in Subh, a similar length in Dhuhr, shorter in 'Asr and Maghrib and medium length in 'Isha'

7. The *sura* in the first *rak'at* should come before that in the second in the Qur'an and be longer than it

8. The well-known form of *ruku'*, prostration and sitting

III. The Prayer

وَفَضَائِلُهَا

رَفْعُ الْيَدَيْنِ عِنْدَ الْإِحْرَامِ حَتَّى تُقَابِلَا الْأُذُنَيْنِ

وَقَوْلُ الْمَأْمُومِ وَالْفَذِّ: رَبَّنَا وَلَكَ الْحَمْدُ

وَالتَّأْمِينُ بَعْدَ الْفَاتِحَةِ لِلْفَذِّ وَالْمَأْمُومِ، وَلَا يَقُولُهَا الْإِمَامُ إِلَّا فِي قِرَاءَةِ السِّرِّ

وَالتَّسْبِيحُ فِي الرُّكُوعِ

وَالدُّعَاءُ فِي السُّجُودِ

وَتَطْوِيلُ الْقِرَاءَةِ فِي الصُّبْحِ وَالظُّهْرِ تَلِيهَا وَتَقْصِيرُهَا فِي الْعَصْرِ وَالْمَغْرِبِ، وَتَوَسُّطُهَا فِي الْعِشَاءِ.

وَتَكُونُ السُّورَةُ الْأُولَى قَبْلَ الثَّانِيَةِ وَأَطْوَلَ مِنْهَا

وَالْهَيْئَةُ الْمَعْلُومَةُ فِي الرُّكُوعِ وَالسُّجُودِ وَالْجُلُوسِ

9. Saying the *qunut* supplication silently before *ruku'* and after the *sura* in the second *rak'at* of Subh, but it is also valid after the *ruku'*

10. The *du'a* after the second *tashahhud*

11. The second *tashahhud* being longer than the first

12. The *salam* said to the right side

14. The movement of the finger during the *tashahhud*

7. Disliked Things in the Prayer

1. Looking about in the prayer

2. Closing the eyes

3. Saying the *basmala* or seeking refuge in the *fard* prayer, but they are permitted in the *nafila*

4. Standing on one foot unless someone is standing for a long time

III. The Prayer

وَالْقُنُوتِ سِرًّا قَبْلَ الرُّكُوعِ وَبَعْدَ السُّورَةِ فِي ثَانِيَةِ الصُّبْحِ

وَيَجُوزُ بَعْدَ الرُّكُوعِ

وَالدُّعَاءُ بَعْدَ التَّشَهُّدِ الثَّانِي

وَيَكُونُ التَّشَهُّدُ الثَّانِي أَطْوَلَ مِنَ الْأَوَّلِ

وَالتَّيَامُنُ بِالسَّلَامِ

وَتَحْرِيكُ السَّبَّابَةِ فِي التَّشَهُّدِ

وَيُكْرَهُ

الِالْتِفَاتُ فِي الصَّلَاةِ

وَتَغْمِيضُ الْعَيْنَيْنِ

وَالْبَسْمَلَةُ وَالتَّعَوُّذُ فِي الْفَرِيضَةِ وَيَجُوزَانِ فِي النَّفْلِ

وَالْوُقُوفُ عَلَى رِجْلٍ وَاحِدَةٍ إِلَّا أَنْ يَطُولَ قِيَامُهُ

5. Having the feet right together

6. Putting a coin or something else in the mouth, or putting anything that might distract you in your pocket, sleeve or on your back

7. Thinking about worldly things and anything else that may distract you from having true humility in your prayer.

Section

There is an immense light in the prayer, with which the hearts of those who pray are illuminated, and it is only obtained by those who have true humility.

When you come to the prayer, you should empty your heart of this world and everything in it and occupy yourself with attentiveness to your Lord for whose sake you are praying. Believe that the prayer entails true humility and self-effacement before Allah, expressed by means of standing, bowing, prostrating, and respecting and esteeming Him through *takbir*, glorification and dhikr.

III. The Prayer

واقْتِرانُ رِجْلَيْهِ

وَجَعْلُ دِرْهَمٍ أَوْ غَيْرِهِ فِي فِيهِ، وَكَذَلِكَ كُلُّ مَا يُشَوِّشُهُ فِي جَيْبِهِ أَوْ كُمِّهِ أَوْ عَلَى ظَهْرِهِ

وَالتَّفَكُّرُ فِي أُمُورِ الدُّنْيَا، وَكُلُّ مَا يَشْغَلُهُ عَنِ الْخُشُوعِ فِي الصَّلَاةِ.

فَصْلٌ

لِلصَّلَاةِ نُورٌ عَظِيمٌ تُشْرِقُ بِهِ قُلُوبُ الْمُصَلِّينَ وَلَا يَنَالُهُ إِلَّا الْخَاشِعُونَ.

فَإِذَا أَتَيْتَ إِلَى الصَّلَاةِ فَفَرِّغْ قَلْبَكَ مِنَ الدُّنْيَا وَمَا فِيهَا، وَاشْتَغِلْ بِمُرَاقَبَةِ مَوْلَاكَ الَّذِي تُصَلِّي لِوَجْهِهِ وَاعْتَقِدْ أَنَّ الصَّلَاةَ خُشُوعٌ وَتَوَاضُعٌ لِلَّهِ سُبْحَانَهُ بِالْقِيَامِ وَالرُّكُوعِ وَالسُّجُودِ وَإِجْلَالٌ وَتَعْظِيمٌ لَهُ بِالتَّكْبِيرِ وَالتَّسْبِيحِ وَالذِّكْرِ.

Take great care of your prayer. It is the greatest of acts of worship. Do not allow Shaytan to play with your heart and distract you from your prayer, so that he obliterates it and deprives you of the pleasure of the lights of the prayer.

You must persevere with maintaining your humility throughout it for it *"precludes indecency and wrongdoing"* (29:45) through the humility you bring to it. And seek help from Allah. He is the Best of Helpers.

Section

There are seven ways in which the obligatory prayer can be done, four of which are obligatory and three recommended.

The obligatory ways are:

1. Firstly standing without support

2. Then standing with support

3. Then sitting without support

4. Then sitting with support.

III. The Prayer

فَحَافِظْ عَلَى صَلَاتِكَ فَإِنَّهَا أَعْظَمُ الْعِبَادَاتِ، وَلَا تَتْرُكِ الشَّيْطَانَ يَلْعَبُ بِقَلْبِكَ وَيَشْغَلُكَ عَنْ صَلَاتِكَ حَتَّى يَطْمِسَ قَلْبَكَ وَيَحْرِمَكَ مِنْ لَذَّةِ أَنْوَارِ الصَّلَاةِ.

فَعَلَيْكَ بِدَوَامِ الْخُشُوعِ فِيهَا فَإِنَّهَا ﴿تَنْهَى عَنِ الْفَحْشَاءِ وَالْمُنْكَرِ﴾ بِسَبَبِ الْخُشُوعِ فِيهَا، فَاسْتَعِنْ بِاللَّهِ إِنَّهُ خَيْرُ مُسْتَعَانٍ.

فَصْلٌ

لِلصَّلَاةِ الْمَفْرُوضَةِ سَبْعَةُ أَحْوَالٍ مُرَتَّبَةٍ تُؤَدَّى عَلَيْهَا أَرْبَعَةٌ مِنْهَا عَلَى الْوُجُوبِ، وَثَلَاثَةٌ عَلَى الِاسْتِحْبَابِ.

أَوَّلُهَا الْقِيَامُ بِغَيْرِ اسْتِنَادٍ

ثُمَّ الْقِيَامُ بِاسْتِنَادٍ

ثُمَّ الْجُلُوسُ بِغَيْرِ اسْتِنَادٍ

ثُمَّ الْجُلُوسُ بِاسْتِنَادٍ

The ruling in respect of the obligatory nature of these four is that when someone is capable of praying in one of these ways and then prays in a lesser way, their prayer is invalidated.

The three recommended ways are for those unable to pray in any of the first four. They are:

1. On the right side

2. On the left side

3. On the back.

With these if someone prays in one of them rather than another, his prayer is not invalidated.

The support which invalidates the prayer of the one who is able to dispense with it is such that, if it fell, he would fall over. If he would not fall when it fell, then it is disliked.

In the case of *nafila* prayers, it is permitted for someone who is able to stand to pray it sitting down, but they only have half the reward of the person standing. It is permitted to begin the prayer sitting and then stand afterwards, or to begin it standing and then sit afterwards, unless

III. The Prayer

فَالتَّرْتِيبُ بَيْنَ هَذِهِ الْأَرْبَعَةِ عَلَى الْوُجُوبِ إِذَا قَدَرَ عَلَى حَالَةٍ مِنْهَا وَصَلَّى بِحَالَةٍ دُونَهَا بَطَلَتْ صَلَاتُهُ

وَالثَّلَاثَةُ الَّتِي عَلَى الِاسْتِحْبَابِ هِيَ: أَنْ يُصَلِّيَ الْعَاجِزُ عَنْ هَذِهِ الثَّلَاثَةِ الْمَذْكُورَةِ

عَلَى جَنْبِهِ الْأَيْمَنِ

ثُمَّ عَلَى الْأَيْسَرِ

ثُمَّ عَلَى ظَهْرِهِ

فَإِنْ خَالَفَ فِي الثَّلَاثَةِ لَمْ تَبْطُلْ صَلَاتُهُ

وَالِاسْتِنَادُ الَّذِي تَبْطُلُ بِهِ صَلَاةُ الْقَادِرِ عَلَى تَرْكِهِ هُوَ الَّذِي يَسْقُطُ بِسُقُوطِهِ، وَإِنْ كَانَ لَا يَسْقُطُ بِسُقُوطِهِ فَهُوَ مَكْرُوهٌ.

وَأَمَّا النَّافِلَةُ فَيَجُوزُ لِلْقَادِرِ عَلَى الْقِيَامِ أَنْ يُصَلِّيَهَا جَالِسًا، وَلَهُ نِصْفُ أَجْرِ الْقَائِمِ. وَيَجُوزُ أَنْ يَدْخُلَهَا جَالِسًا وَيَقُومُ بَعْدَ ذَلِكَ أَوْ يَدْخُلَهَا قَائِمًا وَيَجْلِسُ بَعْدَ ذَلِكَ إِلَّا أَنْ يَدْخُلَهَا بِنِيَّةِ الْقِيَامِ فِيهَا فَيَمْتَنِعُ جُلُوسُهُ بَعْدَ ذَلِكَ.

it was started with the intention of standing, in which case it is forbidden to sit after that.

8. Making up Prayers

Missed prayers must be made up and it is not lawful to be negligent about doing that. Someone who makes up five days worth of prayers on each day is not considered negligent. They should be made up in the same form that they were missed, so if the prayer was missed while someone was resident, it must be made up as a resident prayer and if it was a prayer missed while travelling, it must be made up as a travelling prayer, no matter whether, at the time it is made up, the person is resident or on a journey.

The correct order between two current prayers is obligatory as it is between a few missed prayers when the person remembers. A few means four prayers or less.

If someone owes four or less prayers, they must pray them before the prayer of the time they are in even if that entails missing the time of that prayer. It is permitted to make up prayers at any time. Someone with missed prayers does not

III. The Prayer

فَصْلٌ

يَجِبُ قَضَاءُ مَا فِي الذِّمَّةِ مِنْ الصَّلَوَاتِ وَلَا يَحِلُّ التَّفْرِيطُ فِيهَا، وَمَنْ صَلَّى كُلَّ يَوْمٍ خَمْسَةَ أَيَّامٍ فَلَيْسَ بِمُفَرِّطٍ وَيَقْضِيهَا عَلَى نَحْوِ مَا فَاتَتْهُ إِنْ كَانَتْ حَضَرِيَّةً قَضَاهَا حَضَرِيَّةً، وَإِنْ كَانَتْ سَفَرِيَّةً قَضَاهَا سَفَرِيَّةً سَوَاءٌ كَانَ حِينَ الْقَضَاءِ فِي حَضَرٍ أَوْ سَفَرٍ.

وَالتَّرْتِيبُ بَيْنَ الْحَاضِرَتَيْنِ وَبَيْنَ يَسِيرِ الْفَوَائِتِ مَعَ الْحَاضِرَةِ وَاجِبٌ مَعَ الذِّكْرِ، وَالْيَسِيرُ أَرْبَعُ صَلَوَاتٍ فَأَدْنَى.

وَمَنْ كَانَتْ عَلَيْهِ أَرْبَعُ صَلَوَاتٍ فَأَقَلُّ صَلَّاهَا قَبْلَ الْحَاضِرَةِ وَلَوْ خَرَجَ وَقْتُهَا، وَيَجُوزُ الْقَضَاءُ فِي كُلِّ وَقْتٍ. وَلَا يَتَنَفَّلُ مَنْ عَلَيْهِ الْقَضَاءُ وَلَا يُصَلِّي الضُّحَى وَلَا قِيَامَ رَمَضَانَ وَلَا

do any *nafila* connected to the prayers they are making up, nor do they do the Duha prayer or Ramadan night prayers. The only extra prayers they are permitted to do are the *shafʿ* and *witr*, Fajr, the two ʿeids, the eclipse prayer and the rain prayer.

It is permitted for people who have prayers to make up to pray in a group prayer if their prayer is the same one.

If anyone forgets the number of prayers they have missed, they should pray a number sufficient to leave no doubt that they have prayed enough.

9. On Forgetfulness

Prostration on account of forgetfulness in the prayer is sunna.

For something left out, there are two prostrations before the *salam* after the *tashahhud*, followed by another *tashahhud*, followed by the *salam*.

For something added, there are two prostrations after the *salam*, with a *tashahhud* after them followed by another *salam*.

III. The Prayer

يَجُوزُ لَهُ إِلَّا الشَّفْعُ وَالْوَتْرُ وَالْفَجْرُ وَالْعِيدَانِ وَالْخُسُوفُ وَالِاسْتِسْقَاءُ.

وَيَجُوزُ لِمَنْ عَلَيْهِمُ الْقَضَاءُ أَنْ يُصَلُّوا جَمَاعَةً إِذَا اسْتَوَتْ صَلَاتُهُمْ.

وَمَنْ نَسِيَ عَدَدَ مَا عَلَيْهِ مِنْ الْقَضَاءِ صَلَّى عَدَدًا لَا يَبْقَى مَعَهُ شَكٌّ.

بَابٌ فِي السَّهْوِ

وَسُجُودُ السَّهْوِ فِي الصَّلَاةِ سُنَّةٌ.

فَلِلنُّقْصَانِ سَجْدَتَانِ قَبْلَ السَّلَامِ بَعْدَ تَمَامِ التَّشَهُّدَيْنِ يَزِيدُ بَعْدَهُمَا تَشَهُّدًا آخَرَ.

وَلِلزِّيَادَةِ سَجْدَتَانِ بَعْدَ السَّلَامِ يَتَشَهَّدُ بَعْدَهُمَا وَيُسَلِّمُ تَسْلِيمَةً أُخْرَى.

Anyone who both adds and leaves something out should prostrate before the *salam*.

Anyone who forgets the prostration before the *salam* until they have already said the *salam* should prostrate if it is soon afterwards. If it is a long time afterwards, or they have left the mosque, the prostration is invalid and the prayer is also invalidated it if it was on account of missing three or more sunnas. Otherwise it is not invalidated.

If someone forgets the prostration after the *salam*, they should do it, even if a year has elapsed.

If someone omits an obligatory element of the prayer, the prostration is not adequate to make up for its omission.

There is no prostration on account of omitting a meritorious part of the prayer.

There is no prostration before the *salam* except for the omission of two or more sunnas.

If it is a single sunna, there is no prostration for it, except for wrongly reciting silently or aloud. If someone does an outloud prayer silently, they should prostrate before the *salam*, and if someone does the silent prayer aloud, they should prostrate after the *salam*.

III. The Prayer

وَمَنْ نَقَصَ وَزَادَ سَجَدَ قَبْلَ السَّلَامِ.

وَمَنْ نَسِيَ السُّجُودَ الْقَبْلِيَّ حَتَّى سَلَّمَ سَجَدَ إِنْ كَانَ قَرِيبًا، وَإِنْ طَالَ أَوْ خَرَجَ مِنَ الْمَسْجِدِ بَطَلَ السُّجُودُ وَتَبْطُلُ الصَّلَاةُ مَعَهُ إِنْ كَانَ عَلَى ثَلَاثِ سُنَنٍ أَوْ أَكْثَرَ مِنْ ذَلِكَ وَإِلَّا فَلَا تَبْطُلُ.

وَمَنْ نَسِيَ السُّجُودَ الْبَعْدِيَّ سَجَدَهُ وَلَوْ بَعْدَ عَامٍ.

وَمَنْ نَقَصَ فَرِيضَةً فَلَا يُجْزِيهِ السُّجُودُ عَنْهَا.

وَمَنْ نَقَصَ الْفَضَائِلَ فَلَا سُجُودَ عَلَيْهِ.

وَلَا يَكُونُ السُّجُودُ الْقَبْلِيُّ إِلَّا لِتَرْكِ سُنَّتَيْنِ فَأَكْثَرَ.

وَأَمَّا السُّنَّةُ الْوَاحِدَةُ فَلَا سُجُودَ لَهَا إِلَّا السِّرَّ وَالْجَهْرَ، فَمَنْ أَسَرَّ فِي الْجَهْرِ سَجَدَ قَبْلَ السَّلَامِ، وَمَنْ جَهَرَ فِي السِّرِّ سَجَدَ بَعْدَ السَّلَامِ.

If someone speaks inadvertently they must prostrate after the *salam*.

If someone says the *salam* inadvertently after two *rak'ats*, they must prostrate after the *salam*.

If someone adds one or two *rak'ats* to the prayer, they prostrate after the *salam*. If someone doubles the number of *rak'ats* in the prayer, the prayer is invalidated.

If someone is unsure about having completed the prayer, they do what they are unsure about.

Doubt about omitting something should be resolved. So if someone is unsure about whether they have done a *rak'at* or a prostration or not, they do it and prostrate after the *salam*.

If someone is unsure about the *salam*, they say the *salam*, if it is soon afterwards, and owe no prostration. But if a long time has passed, their prayer is invalidated.

Someone subject to whisperings ignores the whispering and does not do what they are unsure about, but they should prostrate after the *salam*, whether the doubt is about addition or omission.

If someone does the *qunut* aloud, they do not prostrate for it, but it is disliked to do that deliberately.

III. The Prayer

وَمَنْ تَكَلَّمَ سَاهِياً سَجَدَ بَعْدَ السَّلَامِ.

وَمَنْ سَلَّمَ مِنْ رَكْعَتَيْنِ سَاهِياً سَجَدَ بَعْدَ السَّلَامِ.

وَمَنْ زَادَ فِي الصَّلَاةِ رَكْعَةً أَوْ رَكْعَتَيْنِ سَجَدَ بَعْدَ السَّلَامِ

وَمَنْ زَادَ فِي الصَّلَاةِ مِثْلَهَا بَطَلَتْ.

وَمَنْ شَكَّ فِي كَمَالِ صَلَاتِهِ أَتَى بِمَا شَكَّ فِيهِ.

وَالشَّكُّ فِي النُّقْصَانِ كَتَحَقُّقِهِ. فَمَنْ شَكَّ فِي رَكْعَةٍ أَوْ سَجْدَةٍ أَتَى بِهَا وَسَجَدَ بَعْدَ السَّلَامِ.

وَإِنْ شَكَّ فِي السَّلَامِ سَلَّمَ إِنْ كَانَ قَرِيباً وَلَا سُجُودَ عَلَيْهِ، وَإِنْ طَالَ بَطَلَتْ صَلَاتُهُ.

وَالْمُوَسْوَسُ يَتْرُكُ الْوَسْوَسَةَ مِنْ قَلْبِهِ، وَلَا يَأْتِي بِمَا شَكَّ فِيهِ وَلَكِنْ يَسْجُدُ بَعْدَ السَّلَامِ سَوَاءٌ شَكَّ فِي زِيَادَةٍ أَوْ نُقْصَانٍ.

وَمَنْ جَهَرَ فِي الْقُنُوتِ فَلَا سُجُودَ عَلَيْهِ وَلَكِنَّهُ يُكْرَهُ عَمْدُهُ.

If someone adds a *sura* in the last two *rak'ats*, they do not prostrate for it.

If someone hears Muhammad ﷺ mentioned while they are praying and says the prayer on him, they owe nothing, whether it was inadvertent or deliberate, standing or sitting.

If someone recites two or more *suras* in one *rak'at*, or goes from one *sura* to another, or goes into *ruku'* before completing the *sura*, they owe nothing for any of that.

If someone makes a gesture with his hand or head in the prayer he owes nothing.

If someone repeats the Fatiha inadvertently, they should prostrate before the *salam*. If they do it deliberately, it is probable that their prayer is invalid.

If someone remembers not reciting the *sura* after they have gone into *ruku'* they do not go back to do it.

If someone remembers that they should have been reciting silently or aloud before going into *ruku'*, they should repeat the recitation. If it

III. The Prayer

ومَنْ زَادَ السُّورَةَ فِي الرَّكْعَتَيْنِ الْأَخِيرَتَيْنِ فَلَا سُجُودَ عَلَيْهِ.

ومَنْ سَمِعَ ذِكْرَ مُحَمَّدٍ صَلَّى اللهُ عَلَيْهِ وَسَلَّمَ وهوَ فِي الصَّلَاةِ فَصَلَّى عَلَيْهِ فَلَا شَيْءَ عَلَيْهِ، سَوَاءٌ كَانَ سَاهِيًا أَوْ عَامِدًا أَوْ قَائِمًا أَوْ جَالِسًا.

ومَنْ قَرَأَ سُورَتَيْنِ فَأَكْثَرَ فِي رَكْعَةٍ وَاحِدَةٍ أَوْ خَرَجَ مِنْ سُورَةٍ إِلَى سُورَةٍ، أَوْ رَكَعَ قَبْلَ تَمَامِ السُّورَةِ فَلَا شَيْءَ عَلَيْهِ فِي جَمِيعِ ذَلِكَ.

ومَنْ أَشَارَ فِي صَلَاتِهِ بِيَدِهِ أَوْ رَأْسِهِ فَلَا شَيْءَ عَلَيْهِ.

ومَنْ كَرَّرَ الْفَاتِحَةَ سَاهِيًا سَجَدَ بَعْدَ السَّلَامِ، وإِنْ كَانَ عَامِدًا فَالظَّاهِرُ الْبُطْلَانُ.

ومَنْ تَذَكَّرَ السُّورَةَ بَعْدَ انْحِنَائِهِ إِلَى الرُّكُوعِ فَلَا يَرْجِعُ إِلَيْهَا.

ومَنْ تَذَكَّرَ السِّرَّ أَوِ الْجَهْرَ قَبْلَ الرُّكُوعِ أَعَادَ الْقِرَاءَةَ، فَإِنْ كَانَ ذَلِكَ فِي السُّورَةِ وَحْدَهَا أَعَادَهَا وَلَا سُجُودَ عَلَيْهِ،

was only the *sura*, they should repeat it and not prostrate for it. If it was the Fatiha, they should repeat it and prostrate after the *salam*. If someone has already gone into *rukuʻ*, they prostrate for failing to recite aloud before the *salam*, and for not being silent after the *salam*, whether that was in the Fatiha or just the *sura*.

If someone laughs in the prayer, their prayer is invalidated, no matter whether it was inadvertent or intentional. Only a heedless person or someone playing around laughs in the prayer.

When believers stand for the prayer, they should turn with their hearts from everything except Allah Almighty and forsake this world and all it contains, so that they are present with their hearts before the Majesty of Allah Almighty and His Immensity, and their hearts tremble and their souls are filled with terror and awe of Allah. This is the prayer of the godfearing.

Nothing is owed for smiling.

The weeping of the humble in the prayer is excused.

Anyone who hears someone say something owes nothing.

III. The Prayer

وَإِنْ كَانَ فِي الْفَاتِحَةِ أَعَادَهَا وَسَجَدَ بَعْدَ السَّلَامِ، وَإِنْ فَاتَ بِالرُّكُوعِ سَجَدَ لِتَرْكِ الْجَهْرِ قَبْلَ السَّلَامِ وَلِتَرْكِ السِّرِّ بَعْدَ السَّلَامِ سَوَاءٌ كَانَ مِنَ الْفَاتِحَةِ أَوِ السُّورَةِ وَحْدَهَا.

وَمَنْ ضَحِكَ فِي الصَّلَاةِ بَطَلَتْ سَوَاءٌ كَانَ سَاهِيًا أَوْ عَامِدًا، وَلَا يَضْحَكُ فِي صَلَاتِهِ إِلَّا غَافِلٌ مُتَلَاعِبٌ.

وَالْمُؤْمِنُ إِذَا قَامَ لِلصَّلَاةِ أَعْرَضَ بِقَلْبِهِ عَنْ كُلِّ مَا سِوَى اللهِ سُبْحَانَهُ وَتَرَكَ الدُّنْيَا وَمَا فِيهَا، حَتَّى يُحْضِرَ بِقَلْبِهِ جَلَالَ اللهِ سُبْحَانَهُ وَعَظَمَتَهُ، وَيَرْتَعِدَ قَلْبُهُ وَتَرْهَبَ نَفْسُهُ مِنْ هَيْبَةِ اللهِ جَلَّ جَلَالُهُ، فَهَذِهِ صَلَاةُ الْمُتَّقِينَ.

وَلَا شَيْءَ عَلَيْهِ فِي التَّبَسُّمِ.
وَبُكَاءُ الْخَاشِعِ فِي الصَّلَاةِ مُغْتَفَرٌ.
وَمَنْ أَنْصَتَ لِمُتَحَدِّثٍ قَلِيلًا فَلَا شَيْءَ عَلَيْهِ.

If someone stands up after two *rak'ats* before sitting and remembers before their hands and knees have left the ground, they sit and no prostration is owed by them. If they have left the ground, they continue and do not go back but prostate before the *salam*. If they do go back after leaving the ground and standing up, whether out of forgetfulness or intentionally, their prayer is valid and they should prostrate after the *salam*.

Anyone who blows[3] in his prayer inadvertently should prostrate after the *salam*. If anyone does it deliberately, his prayer is invalidated.

If someone sneezes in the prayer, they should not say "*al-hamdulillah*", nor should they reply to anyone who blesses them nor bless someone else who sneezes. If, however, someone does praise Allah, they owe nothing.

Anyone who yawns in the prayer should put their hand over their mouth and no one should spit except into their garment and without making any noise.

---

3 This involves expelling the breath loudly.

III. The Prayer

وَمَنْ قَامَ مِنْ رَكْعَتَيْنِ قَبْلَ الْجُلُوسِ، فَإِنْ تَذَكَّرَ قَبْلَ أَنْ يُفَارِقَ الْأَرْضَ بِيَدَيْهِ وَرُكْبَتَيْهِ رَجَعَ إِلَى الْجُلُوسِ وَلَا يَسْجُدُ عَلَيْهِ، وَإِنْ فَارَقَهَا تَمَادَى وَلَمْ يَرْجِعْ وَسَجَدَ قَبْلَ السَّلَامِ، وَإِنْ رَجَعَ بَعْدَ الْمُفَارَقَةِ وَبَعْدَ الْقِيَامِ سَاهِيًا أَوْ عَامِدًا صَحَّتْ صَلَاتُهُ وَسَجَدَ بَعْدَ السَّلَامِ.

وَمَنْ نَفَخَ فِي صَلَاتِهِ سَاهِيًا سَجَدَ بَعْدَ السَّلَامِ، وَإِنْ كَانَ عَامِدًا بَطَلَتْ صَلَاتُهُ.

وَمَنْ عَطَسَ فِي صَلَاتِهِ فَلَا يَشْتَغِلُ بِالْحَمْدِ وَلَا يَرُدُّ عَلَى مَنْ شَمَّتَهُ وَلَا يُشَمِّتُ عَاطِسًا، فَإِنْ حَمِدَ اللَّهَ فَلَا شَيْءَ عَلَيْهِ.

وَمَنْ تَثَاءَبَ فِي الصَّلَاةِ سَدَّ فَاهُ، وَلَا يَنْفُثُ إِلَّا فِي ثَوْبِهِ مِنْ غَيْرِ إِخْرَاجِ حُرُوفٍ.

If someone has a doubt about their purity or having an impurity on them and then, after reflecting a little during the prayer, become sure that they are pure, they owe nothing.

If someone looks about inadvertently in their prayer, they owe nothing. If they do it deliberately it is disliked. If they turn their back to *qibla*, they break the prayer.

If someone prays wearing silk or gold, or steals during the prayer, or looks at something forbidden, they are sinful but their prayer is valid.

If someone errs in their recitation by using a word which is not the Qur'an, they should prostrate after the *salam*. If it is in the Qur'an, they do not prostrate for it unless they have altered the phrase or destroyed the meaning, and then they should prostrate after the *salam*.

Someone who dozes off in the prayer does not owe a prostration. But if they fall into a heavy sleep, they must do *wudu'* and repeat the prayer.

The groan of a sick person is excused as is clearing the throat. Doing that to gain attention is disliked but the prayer is not invalidated by it.

III. The Prayer

وَمَنْ شَكَّ فِي حَدَثٍ أَوْ نَجَاسَةٍ فَتَفَكَّرَ فِي صَلَاتِهِ قَلِيلًا، ثُمَّ تَيَقَّنَ الطَّهَارَةَ فَلَا شَيْءَ عَلَيْهِ.

وَمَنِ الْتَفَتَ فِي الصَّلَاةِ سَاهِيًا فَلَا شَيْءَ عَلَيْهِ، وَإِنْ تَعَمَّدَ فَهُوَ مَكْرُوهٌ، وَإِنِ اسْتَدْبَرَ الْقِبْلَةَ قَطَعَ الصَّلَاةَ.

وَمَنْ صَلَّى بِحَرِيرٍ أَوْ ذَهَبٍ أَوْ سَرَقَ فِي الصَّلَاةِ أَوْ نَظَرَ مُحَرَّمًا فَهُوَ عَاصٍ وَصَلَاتُهُ صَحِيحَةٌ.

وَمَنْ غَلِطَ فِي الْقِرَاءَةِ بِكَلِمَةٍ مِنْ غَيْرِ الْقُرْآنِ سَجَدَ بَعْدَ السَّلَامِ، وَإِنْ كَانَتْ مِنَ الْقُرْآنِ فَلَا سُجُودَ عَلَيْهِ إِلَّا أَنْ يَتَغَيَّرَ اللَّفْظُ أَوْ يَفْسُدَ الْمَعْنَى فَيَسْجُدَ بَعْدَ السَّلَامِ.

وَمَنْ نَعَسَ فِي الصَّلَاةِ فَلَا سُجُودَ عَلَيْهِ، وَإِنْ ثَقُلَ نَوْمُهُ أَعَادَ الصَّلَاةَ وَالْوُضُوءَ.

وَأَنِينُ الْمَرِيضِ مُغْتَفَرٌ وَالتَّنَحْنُحُ لِلضَّرُورَةِ مُغْتَفَرٌ، وَلِلْإِفْهَامِ مُنْكَرٌ وَلَا تَبْطُلُ الصَّلَاةُ بِهِ.

If someone calls out to someone and they say, "*subhan'allah*," that is disliked, but their prayer is valid.

If someone gets stuck in their recitation and no one prompts them, they should go on from that *ayat* and recite the one after it. If that is impossible for them, they should go into *ruku'*. They should not look at a copy of the Qur'an, unless it is a question of the Fatiha, in which case they must complete it by looking at a copy of the Qur'an or something else.

If someone omits a single *ayat* of the Fatiha, they must prostrate before the *salam*. If it is more than that, the prayer is invalidated.

Helping anyone other than the imam in recitation invalidates the prayer, and no one should even help the imam unless he is waiting for it or has altered the meaning.

If someone thinks a little about worldly matters in the prayer, their reward is decreased but their prayer is not invalidated.

If someone pushes away someone who walks in front of him, or prostrates on the side of his forehead, or prostrates on a layer or two of his turban, they owe nothing.

III. The Prayer

وَمَنْ نَادَاهُ أَحَدٌ فَقَالَ لَهُ: سُبْحَانَ اللَّهِ كُرِهَ وَصَحَّتْ صَلَاتُهُ.

وَمَنْ وَقَفَ فِي الْقِرَاءَةِ وَلَمْ يَفْتَحْ عَلَيْهِ أَحَدٌ تَرَكَ تِلْكَ الْآيَةَ وَقَرَأَ مَا بَعْدَهَا، فَإِنْ تَعَذَّرَتْ عَلَيْهِ رَكَعَ. وَلَا يَنْظُرُ مُصْحَفًا بَيْنَ يَدَيْهِ إِلَّا أَنْ يَكُونَ فِي الْفَاتِحَةِ فَلَا بُدَّ مِنْ كَمَالِهَا بِمُصْحَفٍ أَوْ غَيْرِهِ.

فَإِنْ تَرَكَ مِنْهَا آيَةً سَجَدَ قَبْلَ السَّلَامِ، وَإِنْ كَانَ أَكْثَرَ بَطَلَتْ صَلَاتُهُ.

وَمَنْ فَتَحَ عَلَى غَيْرِ إِمَامِهِ بَطَلَتْ صَلَاتُهُ. وَلَا يَفْتَحْ عَلَى إِمَامِهِ إِلَّا أَنْ يَنْتَظِرَ الْفَتْحَ أَوْ يُفْسِدَ الْمَعْنَى.

وَمَنْ جَالَ فِكْرُهُ قَلِيلًا فِي أُمُورِ الدُّنْيَا نَقَصَ ثَوَابُهُ وَلَمْ تَبْطُلْ صَلَاتُهُ.

وَمَنْ دَفَعَ الْمَاشِيَ بَيْنَ يَدَيْهِ أَوْ سَجَدَ عَلَى شِقِّ جَبْهَتِهِ أَوْ سَجَدَ عَلَى طَيَّةٍ أَوْ طَيَّتَيْنِ مِنْ عِمَامَتِهِ فَلَا شَيْءَ عَلَيْهِ.

Nor is there anything owed for involuntary reflux or belching in the prayer.

The forgetfulness of the follower is borne by the imam, unless it is the omission of an obligatory element of the prayer.

If a follower forgets where he is or dozes off or is prevented by the crowd from doing *ruku'* and it is not in the first *rak'at*, and he feels he can catch the imam before he rises from the second prostration, he does *ruku'* and joins him. If he does not feel he can catch the imam, he leaves out the *ruku'* and follows the imam and he makes up that *rak'at* there and then after the the imam has said the *salam*.

If a follower is distracted from prostration or is prevented by crowding or dozes off until the imam stands for the next *rak'at*, he prostrates, if he feels able to catch the imam before he goes into *ruku'*. Otherwise he leaves it out and follows the imam and then makes up another *rak'at*. When he makes up the *rak'at*, he owes no prostration unless he is unsure about having bowed or prostrated.

If a scorpion or snake approaches someone

III. The Prayer

وَلَا شَيْءَ فِي غَلَبَةِ الْقَيْءِ وَالْقَلْسِ فِي الصَّلَاةِ.

وَسَهْوُ الْمَأْمُومِ يَحْمِلُهُ الْإِمَامُ إِلَّا أَنْ يَكُونَ مِنْ نَقْصِ الْفَرِيضَةِ.

وَإِذَا سَهَا الْمَأْمُومُ أَوْ نَعَسَ أَوْ زُوحِمَ عَنِ الرُّكُوعِ وَهُوَ فِي غَيْرِ الْأُولَى، فَإِنْ طَمِعَ فِي إِدْرَاكِ الْإِمَامِ قَبْلَ رَفْعِهِ مِنَ السَّجْدَةِ الثَّانِيَةِ رَكَعَ وَلَحِقَهُ، وَإِنْ لَمْ يَطْمَعْ تَرَكَ الرُّكُوعَ وَتَبِعَ إِمَامَهُ وَقَضَى رَكْعَةً فِي مَوْضِعِهَا بَعْدَ سَلَامِ إِمَامِهِ.

وَإِنْ سَهَا عَنِ السُّجُودِ أَوْ زُوحِمَ أَوْ نَعَسَ حَتَّى قَامَ الْإِمَامُ إِلَى رَكْعَةٍ أُخْرَى سَجَدَ إِنْ طَمِعَ فِي إِدْرَاكِ الْإِمَامِ قَبْلَ الرُّكُوعِ وَإِلَّا تَرَكَهُ وَتَبِعَ الْإِمَامَ وَقَضَى رَكْعَةً أُخْرَى أَيْضًا، وَحَيْثُ قَضَى الرَّكْعَةَ فَلَا سُجُودَ عَلَيْهِ إِلَّا أَنْ يَكُونَ شَاكًّا فِي الرُّكُوعِ أَوِ السُّجُودِ.

وَمَنْ جَاءَتْهُ عَقْرَبٌ أَوْ حَيَّةٌ فَقَتَلَهَا فَلَا شَيْءَ عَلَيْهِ إِلَّا أَنْ

and they kill it, they owe nothing, unless they take a long time over it or turn their back on *qibla*, which breaks the prayer.

If someone is unsure about whether they are in the *witr* or the second *rak'at* of the *shaf'*, they consider it to be the second *rak'at* of the *shaf'* and prostrate after the *salam* and then do the *witr*.

If someone speaks inadvertently between the *shaf'* and the *witr*, they owe nothing. If it is intentional, it is disliked but nothing is owed.

Anyone who arrives late and catches less than one *rak'at* with the imam should not do any extra prostrations with him, whether they are before or after the *salam*. If they do prostrate with the imam, their prayer is invalidated. Anyone who catches a full *rak'at* or more does the extra prostration before the *salam* with the imam but delays the one after the *salam* until they have finished their own prayer and then prostrates after the *salam*. If they prostrate intentionally with the imam, their prayer is invalidated. If they prostrate inadvertently, they should prostrate after the *salam*.

Anyone who arrives late and makes a mistake in the prayer after the *salam* of the imam is like

III. The Prayer

يَطُولَ فِعْلُهُ أَوْ يَسْتَدِيرَ الْقِبْلَةَ فَإِنَّهُ يَقْطَعُ.

وَمَنْ شَكَّ هَلْ هُوَ فِي الْوِتْرِ أَوْ فِي ثَانِيَةِ الشَّفْعِ جَعَلَهَا ثَانِيَةَ الشَّفْعِ وَسَجَدَ بَعْدَ السَّلَامِ ثُمَّ أَوْتَرَ.

وَمَنْ تَكَلَّمَ بَيْنَ الشَّفْعِ وَالْوِتْرِ سَاهِيًا فَلَا شَيْءَ عَلَيْهِ، وَإِنْ كَانَ عَامِدًا كُرِهَ وَلَا شَيْءَ عَلَيْهِ.

وَالْمَسْبُوقُ إِنْ أَدْرَكَ مَعَ الْإِمَامِ أَقَلَّ مِنْ رَكْعَةٍ فَلَا يَسْجُدُ مَعَهُ لَا قَبْلِيًّا وَلَا بَعْدِيًّا فَإِنْ سَجَدَ مَعَهُ بَطَلَتْ صَلَاتُهُ وَإِنْ أَدْرَكَ رَكْعَةً كَامِلَةً أَوْ أَكْثَرَ سَجَدَ مَعَهُ الْقَبْلِيَّ وَأَخَّرَ الْبَعْدِيَّ حَتَّى يُتِمَّ صَلَاتَهُ فَيَسْجُدُ بَعْدَ سَلَامِهِ، فَإِنْ سَجَدَ مَعَ الْإِمَامِ عَامِدًا بَطَلَتْ صَلَاتُهُ وَإِنْ كَانَ سَاهِيًا سَجَدَ بَعْدَ السَّلَامِ.

وَإِنْ سَهَا الْمَسْبُوقُ بَعْدَ سَلَامِ الْإِمَامِ فَهُوَ كَالْمُصَلِّي وَحْدَهُ

someone praying alone. If someone owes a prostration after the *salam* for a mistake by the imam, and one before the *salam* for their own mistake, the one before the *salam* suffices for both.

Anyone who forgets to do *ruku'* and remembers while in prostration should stand up again and it is recommended for them to repeat some of the recitation and then do *ruku'* and prostrate after the *salam*.

Anyone who forgets one prostration and remembers after they have stood up should sit back down and prostrate. However, if they have been sitting before standing up, they should not sit down again.

Anyone who forgets two prostrations goes into prostration without sitting. In all these cases there is a prostration after the *salam*.

Anyone who remembers missing a prostration after rising from the next *ruku'* continues in their prayer and does not go back and do it. They just discount that *rak'at*, add a *rak'at* in its place, building on what they have done, and prostrate before the *salam* as long as it was in one of the first two *rak'ats* and they remember after completing

III. The Prayer

وَإِذَا تَرَتَّبَ عَلَى الْمَسْبُوقِ بَعْدِيٌّ مِنْ جِهَةِ إِمَامِهِ وَقَبْلِيٌّ مِنْ جِهَةِ نَفْسِهِ أَجْزَأَهُ الْقَبْلِيُّ.

وَمَنْ نَسِيَ الرُّكُوعَ وَتَذَكَّرَهُ فِي السُّجُودِ رَجَعَ قَائِمًا، وَيُسْتَحَبُّ لَهُ أَنْ يُعِيدَ شَيْئًا مِنَ الْقِرَاءَةِ ثُمَّ يَرْكَعُ وَيَسْجُدُ بَعْدَ السَّلَامِ.

وَمَنْ نَسِيَ سَجْدَةً وَاحِدَةً وَتَذَكَّرَهَا بَعْدَ قِيَامِهِ رَجَعَ جَالِسًا وَسَجَدَهَا إِلَّا أَنْ يَكُونَ قَدْ جَلَسَ قَبْلَ الْقِيَامِ فَلَا يُعِيدُ الْجُلُوسَ.

وَمَنْ نَسِيَ سَجْدَتَيْنِ خَرَّ سَاجِدًا وَلَمْ يَجْلِسْ وَيَسْجُدُ فِي جَمِيعِ ذَلِكَ بَعْدَ السَّلَامِ.

وَإِنْ تَذَكَّرَ السُّجُودَ بَعْدَ رَفْعِ رَأْسِهِ مِنَ الرَّكْعَةِ الَّتِي تَلِيهَا تَمَادَى عَلَى صَلَاتِهِ وَلَمْ يَرْجِعْ وَأَلْغَى رَكْعَةَ السَّهْوِ وَزَادَ رَكْعَةً فِي مَوْضِعِهَا بَانِيًا وَسَجَدَ قَبْلَ السَّلَامِ، إِنْ كَانَتْ مِنَ الْأُولَيَيْنِ وَتَذَكَّرَ بَعْدَ عَقْدِ الثَّالِثَةِ، وَبَعْدَ السَّلَامِ إِنْ لَمْ تَكُنْ

the third. They should prostrate after the *salam* if it was not in the first two *rak'ats*, or it was but they remember before completing the third. This is because the *sura* and the sitting were not missed.

If someone says the *salam* while unsure whether their prayer has been completed or not, their prayer is invalidated.

Forgetfulness in prayers which are being made up follows the same ruling as forgetfulness in prayers done on time.

Forgetfulness in the Nafila

Forgetfulness in the *nafila* follows the same ruling as forgetfulness in the *fard* with six exceptions: the Fatiha, the *sura*, silent and loud recitation, adding a *rak'at*, and forgetting one of the pillars if a long time has elapsed.

If someone forgets the Fatiha in a *nafila* prayer and remembers after the *ruku'*, they should continue and prostrate before the *salam*, which is different from the *fard* prayer when they would discount that *rak'at*, add another and continue, and their prostration would, as we said, be the same as that for missing a prostration.

If someone forgets the *sura*, or recites aloud

III. The Prayer

مِنَ الْأُولَيَيْنِ أَوْ كَانَتْ مِنْهُمَا وَتَذَكَّرَ قَبْلَ عَقْدِ الثَّالِثَةِ لِأَنَّ السُّورَةَ وَالْجُلُوسَ لَمْ يَفُوتَا.

وَمَنْ سَلَّمَ شَاكًّا فِي كَمَالِ صَلَاتِهِ بَطَلَتْ صَلَاتُهُ.

وَالسَّهْوُ فِي صَلَاةِ الْقَضَاءِ كَالسَّهْوِ فِي صَلَاةِ الْأَدَاءِ.

وَالسَّهْوُ فِي النَّافِلَةِ كَالسَّهْوِ فِي الْفَرِيضَةِ إِلَّا فِي سِتِّ مَسَائِلَ: الْفَاتِحَةِ وَالسُّورَةِ وَالسِّرِّ وَالْجَهْرِ، وَزِيَادَةِ رَكْعَةٍ وَنِسْيَانِ بَعْضِ الْأَرْكَانِ إِنْ طَالَ.

فَمَنْ نَسِيَ الْفَاتِحَةَ فِي النَّافِلَةِ وَتَذَكَّرَ بَعْدَ الرُّكُوعِ تَمَادَى وَسَجَدَ قَبْلَ السَّلَامِ بِخِلَافِ الْفَرِيضَةِ فَإِنَّهُ يُلْغِي تِلْكَ الرَّكْعَةَ وَيَزِيدُ أُخْرَى وَيَتَمَادَى وَيَكُونُ سُجُودُهُ كَمَا ذَكَرْنَا فِي تَارِكِ السُّجُودِ.

وَمَنْ نَسِيَ السُّورَةَ أَوِ الْجَهْرَ أَوِ السِّرَّ فِي النَّافِلَةِ وَتَذَكَّرَ بَعْدَ

or silently in the *nafila*, and remembers after the *ruku'*, they continue and do not owe any prostration, which again would not be the case in a *fard* prayer.

If someone stands for a third *rak'at* in a *nafila* prayer and they remember before they do *ruku'*, they sit back down and prostrate after the *salam*. If they have completed the third *rak'at*, they continue, adding a fourth, and prostrate before the *salam*. In a *fard* prayer they would go back as soon as they realised and prostrate after the *salam*.

If someone forgets an obligatory element in a *nafila* prayer – such as *ruku'* or prostration – and does not realise until after they have said the *salam*, and a long time has passed, they do not have to repeat it, which is different from the *fard*, which must always be repeated.

Anyone who breaks off from a *nafila* deliberately, or leaves out a *rak'at* or prostration from it deliberately, must always repeat it.

If someone sighs in the prayer they owe nothing unless they articulate a letter.

Forgetfulness on the part of the Imam

If the imam makes a mistake, whether of

III. The Prayer

الرُّكُوعِ تَمَادَى وَلَا سُجُودَ عَلَيْهِ بِخِلَافِ الْفَرِيضَةِ.

وَمَنْ قَامَ إِلَى ثَالِثَةٍ فِي النَّافِلَةِ فَإِنْ تَذَكَّرَ قَبْلَ عَقْدِ الرُّكُوعِ رَجَعَ وَسَجَدَ بَعْدَ السَّلَامِ، وَإِنْ عَقَدَ الثَّالِثَةَ تَمَادَى وَزَادَ الرَّابِعَةَ وَسَجَدَ قَبْلَ السَّلَامِ بِخِلَافِ الْفَرِيضَةِ فَإِنَّهُ يَرْجِعُ مَتَى مَا ذَكَّرَ وَيَسْجُدُ بَعْدَ السَّلَامِ.

وَمَنْ نَسِيَ رُكْنًا مِنَ النَّافِلَةِ كَالرُّكُوعِ أَوِ السُّجُودِ وَلَمْ يَتَذَكَّرْ حَتَّى سَلَّمَ وَطَالَ فَلَا إِعَادَةَ عَلَيْهِ بِخِلَافِ الْفَرِيضَةِ فَإِنَّهُ يُعِيدُهَا أَبَدًا.

وَمَنْ قَطَعَ النَّافِلَةَ عَامِدًا أَوْ تَرَكَ مِنْهَا رَكْعَةً أَوْ سَجْدَةً عَامِدًا أَعَادَهَا أَبَدًا.

وَمَنْ تَنَحْنَحَ فِي صَلَاتِهِ فَلَا شَيْءَ عَلَيْهِ إِلَّا أَنْ يَنْطِقَ بِحُرُوفٍ.

وَإِذَا سَهَا الْإِمَامُ بِنَقْصٍ أَوْ زِيَادَةٍ سَبَّحَ بِهِ الْمَأْمُومُ.

omission or addition, the follower should say "*subhan'allah.*"

If your imam starts getting up after two *rak'ats*, say "*subhan'allah*" and, if he leaves the ground, follow him. But if he sits after the first or third *rak'ats*, stand and do not sit with him. If he prostrates once and leaves out the second prostration, say "*subhan'allah*" and do not stand up with him unless you fear he will go into *ruku'*, in which case you should follow him, but then not sit after that with him, either in the second or fourth *rak'at*. When he says the *salam*, add another *rak'at* in place of the one that was spoiled and then prostrate before the *salam*.

If there are several of you, it would be best to put one of you in front to lead you in completing the prayer.

If the imam adds a third prostration, say "*subhan'allah*" and do not prostrate with him.

If the imam gets up for a fifth *rak'at*, you should follow him if you think he is right or are not sure, but remain seated if you are sure it is extra. If the former sits or the latter stands, their prayer is invalidated in both cases.

If the imam says the *salam* before the end of

III. The Prayer

وَإِذَا قَامَ إِمَامُكَ مِنْ رَكْعَتَيْنِ فَسَبِّحْ بِهِ، فَإِنْ فَارَقَ الْأَرْضَ فَاتْبَعْهُ، وَإِنْ جَلَسَ فِي الْأُولَى أَوْ فِي الثَّالِثَةِ فَقُمْ وَلَا تَجْلِسْ مَعَهُ، وَإِنْ سَجَدَ وَاحِدَةً وَتَرَكَ الثَّانِيَةَ فَسَبِّحْ بِهِ وَلَا تَقُمْ مَعَهُ إِلَّا أَنْ تَخَافَ عَقْدَ رُكُوعِهِ فَاتْبَعْهُ وَلَا تَجْلِسْ بَعْدَ ذَلِكَ مَعَهُ لَا فِي ثَانِيَةٍ وَلَا فِي رَابِعَةٍ، فَإِذَا سَلَّمَ فَزِدْ رَكْعَةً أُخْرَى بَدَلًا مِنَ الرَّكْعَةِ الَّتِي أَلْغَيْتَهَا بَانِيًا وَتَسْجُدُ قَبْلَ السَّلَامِ.

فَإِنْ كُنْتُمْ جَمَاعَةً الْأَفْضَلُ لَكُمْ أَنْ تُقَدِّمُوا وَاحِدًا يُتِمُّ بِكُمْ.

وَإِذَا زَادَ الْإِمَامُ سَجْدَةً ثَالِثَةً فَسَبِّحْ بِهِ وَلَا تَسْجُدْ مَعَهُ.

وَإِذَا قَامَ الْإِمَامُ إِلَى خَامِسَةٍ تَبِعَهُ مَنْ تَيَقَّنَ مُوجِبَهَا أَوْ شَكَّ فِيهِ وَجَلَسَ مَنْ تَيَقَّنَ زِيَادَتَهَا، فَإِنْ جَلَسَ الْأَوَّلُ وَقَامَ الثَّانِي بَطَلَتْ صَلَاتُهُ.

وَإِذَا سَلَّمَ الْإِمَامُ قَبْلَ كَمَالِ الصَّلَاةِ سَبَّحَ بِهِ مَنْ خَلْفَهُ، فَإِنْ

the prayer, say "*subhan'allah*" behind him. If he endorses that, he completes his prayer and prostrates after the *salam*.

If he is unsure about it, he should ask two witnesses and they are allowed to speak concerning that. If he is certain he has completed the prayer, he acts on his certainty and ignores the two witnesses, unless there are a lot of people behind him, in which case he abandons his certainty and defers to them.

III. The Prayer

صَدَقَةُ كُلِّ صَلَاتِهِ وَيَسْجُدُ بَعْدَ السَّلَامِ.

وَإِنْ شَكَّ فِي خَبَرِهِ سَأَلَ عَدْلَيْنِ وَجَازَ لَهُمَا الْكَلَامُ فِي ذَلِكَ، وَإِنْ تَيَقَّنَ الْكَمَالَ عَمِلَ عَلَى يَقِينِهِ وَتَرَكَ الْعَدْلَيْنِ إِلَّا أَنْ يَكْثُرَ النَّاسُ خَلْفَهُ فَيَتْرُكَ يَقِينَهُ وَيَرْجِعَ إِلَيْهِمْ.

www.ingramcontent.com/pod-product-compliance
Lightning Source LLC
Chambersburg PA
CBHW071310040426
42444CB00009B/1954